Bright Boy

Martin Jarvis

A SAMUEL FRENCH ACTING EDITION

SAMUEL FRENCH

FOUNDED 1830

SAMUELFRENCH-LONDON.CO.UK
SAMUELFRENCH.COM

BRIGHT BOY

CAST:
Haddleton
Grey
Dietl
A Waiter

BRIGHT BOY

First produced as a radio play for Radio 4 on January 4th, 1973 with the following cast:

Haddleton	Robin Ellis
Grey	Julian Holloway
Dietl	Sean Arnold
Neutze	Rolf Lefebvre
Tannoy Voice, Fraulein and **Receptionist**	Olwen Griffiths
Desk Clerk and **Waiter**	David Gooderson

Produced by Colin Tucker

Subsequently produced for the BBC World Service in March 1975 with the following cast:

Haddleton	Colin Baker
Grey	Martin Jarvis
Dietl	Michael Wolf
Neutze	Frederick Schiller
Tannoy Voice, Fraulein and **Receptionist**	Sabina Michaels
Desk Clerk and **Waiter**	Andrew Lodge

Produced by Dickon Reed

CARMEN

(Haddleton and Grey's old school song, to the tune of
Deutschland Uber Alles)

Here we stand to sing of honour,
Truth shall be our golden rule.
Let our voices raise the rafters
For the honour of our school.
Honour, honour,
Truth and honour,
For the honour of our school.

When across the world we're scattered
As Old Boys we'll raise the cry:
Honour, honour, truth and honour,
Truth and honour 'til we die.
Honour, honour,
Truth and honour,
Truth and honour 'til we die!

For Rosalind, Toby and Oliver, with love

BRIGHT BOY

*The bar, the restaurant and a bedroom in a Munich hotel. Black-out.
Loud, bouncing Bavarian music is heard. The Lights come up on the
bar. Haddleton, an English business man in his thirties, and Dietl,
a German business man of forty, are seated at the bar with steins of
beer. A third man, Grey, an Englishman in his thirties, is also at the
bar, seated on his own*

As Dietl speaks, the music fades to become background Muzak

Dietl Welcome to München, Roger!
Haddleton Thank you.
Dietl How was your flight?
Haddleton Very smooth. It's good to see you Harald. How are
   things? Everything under control?
Dietl Ja. All goes well. And Roger, Herr Neutze will meet you
   tomorrow!
Haddleton Wunderbar!
Dietl He has considered all the proposals of your firm. He be-
   lieves it might be possible—this er—was ist "verschmelzung"?
Haddleton Merger?
Dietl Ja. This merger.
Haddleton Great. We have the goods—You have the market.
Dietl If we can come to agreements in the next few days, then, as
   you say, we are in business. So—Prosit, Roger!
Haddleton Prosit!

They drink

Dietl And how is business in England?
Haddleton Well you know, not bad. It's like sex—when it's good
   it's wundebar, and when it's bad it's still sehr gut!
Dietl Ha! You have not changed, Roger—this English sense of
   humour!
Haddleton Nor have you, Harald. It really is good to see you
   again.

Dietl I think we have a traditional Bavarian evening. You like to eat something, yes?

Haddleton Oh jawohl!

Dietl Good. Then we go downstairs. They have Bavarian Haxe— the best in Munich. Excuse me please, while I fix a table, and then we go down.

Haddleton Righto.

Dietl goes

Grey speaks from his bar stool without looking up

Grey Guten abend, mein herr.

Haddleton I beg your pardon?

Grey Guten abend—(*turning on his stool*)—good evening.

Haddleton Oh—yes—guten abend.

Grey You've got a shocking memory you know.

Haddleton Have I? (*Looking at him*) Good Lord. Er . . .

Grey (*singing, to the tune of* "*Deutschland Über Alles*")
> Here we stand to sing of honour,
> Truth shall be our golden rule . . .

Haddleton Yes. Of course. School. Er . . .

Grey That's right old boy. School song.

Haddleton "Carmen".

Grey Yes—Carmen. Latin for song. Bloody silly really—a song called song. (*He sings*)
> Let our voices raise the rafters,
> For the honour of our school . . .

Haddleton Good lord.

Grey Haven't you got my name yet? Grey. John Grey. How are you Haddock?

Haddleton Grey. Of course. Well—good lord . . .

Grey Moustache threw you probably?

Haddleton Yes, well—it's a long time ago.

Grey Is it? You're Haddleton. Haddock Haddleton.

Haddleton Haddock! I'd forgotten. Yes. Well—how are you? What on earth are you doing here?

Grey Oh just sitting on the touchline. Eavesdropping.

Haddleton Are you staying here as well?

Grey Oh no. I have a little garret round the corner! They know me here though. One time guest you see. In happier and more prosperous days. I drink here sometimes. Come to lick my wounds, you know.

Haddleton What do you do?

Grey Nothing. At the moment.

Haddleton Oh.

Grey I write for various agencies out here. News you know. Bits of gossip. Send them back to England . . .

Haddleton Well I'm blowed.

Grey "Mad axeman loose in Bavarian forest"—"Whizz kid Haddleton blows into town!" That sort of thing.

Haddleton I see. Things are quiet at present are they?

Grey Not really. I think it's my face old boy. Doesn't really fit. Tends not to anyway. Haven't got the breeding, eh! Well well. It's been a long time Haddock. Fifteen-sixteen years at least— You've just arrived, I gather?

Haddleton Yes, indeed. Just.

Grey And you're here on business.

Haddleton Correct again.

Grey Well I told you I'd been listening in old boy. Dies hard, you know! Your own company, is it?

Haddleton Not yet. We've got good hopes of this little expedition though. You sound as if you're interviewing me.

Grey Ah, you never know. Perhaps you'll give me a good story.

Haddleton I shouldn't think so!

Grey Well I'll keep my fingers crossed for the—merger.

Haddleton Dankeschön.

Grey Ah, you speak German? A German sprekker!

Haddleton Eine kleines bischien! Just "O" level you know.

Grey Ah yes. "O" level. Here's to the Old School. Cheers! (*He raises his glass and drinks*)

Haddleton Cheers.

Pause

Grey Well I must say, Haddock old chap, this is a real turn-up for the book—And you look just as bright-eyed and bushy-tailed as ever. Not still playing rugger surely?

Haddleton Good lord no.

Grey A touch of Executive Squash then at least?

Haddleton Just a touch.

Grey (*laughing*) I thought so. (*He pats his stomach*) Worth it though! I say, do you still wield the willow?

Haddleton What?

Grey Cricket. "Twinkle twinkle little bat", and all that! Do you still play?

Haddleton No, no. I hung my boots up many years ago.

Grey Oh. Shame. Do you remember that match against the County Club and Ground? When you scored a hundred before lunch.

Haddleton (*after a moment*) No. Vaguely.

Grey You're joking! Your first season in the Firsts. Only a fifth-former, but opening the batting for the First Eleven. Of course you remember.

Haddleton Not particularly.

Grey I remember. And I wasn't playing.

Haddleton Do you?

Dietl comes back

Dietl All right. All is fixed. Roger, are you all right?

Grey It's shock, that's all.

Dietl Excuse me?

Grey Bit of a shock. A face from the past.

Dietl Oh? I don't . . . ?

Haddleton Er Harald—this is—I'm sorry, what is your christian name?

Grey (*laughing*) Oh come on now—John. John Grey.

Haddleton Yes. John Grey. Harald Dietl.

Dietl How do you do, Mr Grey.

Grey How do you do. I'm an old friend of Roger's. We've just bumped into each other. We were at school together a hundred years ago. He didn't recognize me. I'm not really sure that he even remembers me. But he's putting up a good show—eh Haddock!

Dietl Haddock? That is fish, no?

Grey That's right. Haddleton. Haddock for short. That's what we used to call you, wasn't it?

Haddleton If you say so.

Dietl I understand. Your nickname, Roger.

Grey That's it.

Dietl And what did they call you Mr Grey?

Grey Oh I didn't have one. No such luck. Only the glossy chaps, like Haddock. He was the bright boy, weren't you. The Five Percenter to end all Five Percenters . . .

Haddleton I'm sorry, I haven't a clue what you're talking about.

Grey The Cream. "You chaps are the top five-per-cent. The cream at the top of the bottle. Best opportunities. Best jobs. Best lives. Leaders of men." Don't you remember old Ding Dong Bell telling us all that—in our first year at the school? He was right, though—wouldn't you say?

Haddleton (*laughing*) Well, of course.

Grey We believed him anyway. Well, I mustn't keep you chaps from your gargantuan repast. Bayerische Haxe eh? (*To Haddleton*) That's veal you know. Roasted over a spit. Well, jolly nice to have met you again, Haddock. Enjoy yourselves.

Dietl Good-bye, Mr Grey.

Grey Auf Wiedersehen!

Grey goes

Dietl Haddock! Was he really at school with you, Roger?

Haddleton You heard what he said.

Dietl But you don't remember him?

Haddleton I don't know. There was a chap—in the same form as me. Could have been him. He was decidedly odd. He once ate the Still Life we were trying to paint.

Dietl Pardon me? Ate the still life?

Haddleton Yes. Four shiny red apples—on the Art Room table. Ate them during the lunch hour—and denied all knowledge of it afterwards.

Dietl Perhaps he was hungry—like me. Are you ready?

Haddleton He shouldn't have been there in the lunch hour anyway. Against the rules. We had to paint them from memory because of him.

Dietl You know—it's funny—I feel I know him from somewhere.

Haddleton Some sort of journalist out here, he said.

Dietl So? I have seen him before. I am sure. Well—Prosit! Drink up, and we go. Bayerische Haxe—very traditional.

Haddleton Prosit!

Dietl And we must try the Doppelkorn bier. That is traditional also.

Haddleton Well—I don't think I want to be too late. We do have work to do tomorrow.

Dietl Oh come on, Roger, what's the matter? Later we can sober up with some weisswurst. And some Pschorr Bier. A very good sober-upper!

Haddleton That's traditional as well is it?

Dietl Ha! That's better. Cheers, Roger.

Haddleton Sorry—I was just thinking about tomorrow.

Dietl Don't worry. Neutze likes your ideas. Everything will go well. You will carry it through.

Haddleton I hope you're right. We've spent a lot of time, money and trouble in setting this up. If it all goes through—Boffo Biz—as they say. If it doesn't—well, that doesn't bear thinking about . . .

Dietl What's happened to all that confidence? You have the best equipment. We need it. We shall be in business. Now come . . .

Haddleton Sure.

Haddleton finishes his beer and they start to go

I don't remember him, you know.

The Lights fade to a Black-out. The bouncing Bavarian music swells up

The following morning. The Lights come up on a table in the hotel dining-room. Haddleton is seated at it

A German Waiter enters

Waiter Morning sir. You like café?

Haddleton Good morning. Yes. Strong please.

Waiter (*pouring*) Yes sir. English breakfast, sir?

Haddleton Oh—yes. Boiled eggs?

Waiter Four minutes, sir?

Haddleton Thank you, yes.

Grey enters

Grey Guten Morgen!

Waiter Guten Morgen, Herr Grey. Wie geht es ihnen?

Grey Morning, Gunter. Gute danke. Gute.

Waiter Café, mein Herr?

Grey Ja, bitte—schwartz, and plenty of it! (*He laughs heartily at himself*). Morning, Haddock. Mind if I join you?

Haddleton Good morning.

Grey (*as he sits*) Lovely clear sky this morning. Or didn't you notice?

Haddleton I thought you only came here to drink?

Grey Oh I thought—a little stroll—such "eine schöne morgen"! I say, do you want that other roll?

Haddleton Help yourself.

Grey Jolly decent of you. Thanks. (*Pause*) You get to bed all right last night?

Haddleton Oh yes.

Grey Jolly good. I say—your stripe's still there.

Haddleton My what?

Grey The stripe. Under your chin.

Haddleton I'm sorry?

Grey House colours. Don't you remember? Each House had a different colour stripe on its tie. Red for Raleigh. Green for Drake. I can see yours now. A ghostly white stripe under the chin. Nelson House. Whiter than white. Correct?

Haddleton I suppose so. It's so long ago . . .

Grey Can you see mine?

Haddleton No, I'm sorry I can't—now if you don't mind—

Grey Yellow. Yellow stripe. Sydney House. Never champions of course. At least, not when I was there. Oh well. The Big Day today . . .

Haddleton eats his roll

How are you feeling about it?

Haddleton I beg your pardon?

Grey Are you nervous?

Haddleton Look, old chap . . .

Grey I remember once seeing you before a match. Shaking with nerves you were. Couldn't believe it was the same old Haddock. After that I could always tell.

Haddleton How interesting.

Grey You used to rub the palms of your hands together. That was the giveaway. Funny, I saw you doing it in the bar last night. Nothing wrong with nerves though. You were the best player in the side—glorious cover-drive you had. (*He flicks his wrist as if making a cricket stroke*)

Haddleton I had no idea I was so impressive . . .

Grey Oh you were bloody marvellous all round. Remember old Rags saying to you about some essay "I've got a bone to pick with you, Haddleton . . ."?

Haddleton I don't even remember "old Rags". Sounds rather disgusting.

Grey And you said "Pick away, sir!" And we all laughed like billy-o. And old Rags laughed too. You remember Rags— Mr R. A. Glynne-Smith—R-A-G-S! Marvellous knack you had. Popular with the masters as well as the boys.

Haddleton drinks his coffee

And the time old Treacle-pants whacked you for talking in class. Gave you five whackeroos, my God, and you took 'em without a murmur. When you got up he said "Nobly taken, Haddleton!" And you replied "Nobly given, sir!" Bloody marvellous! Oh yes, old Haddock could get away with murder! But you wound up with a purple gown didn't you? Prefect!

Haddleton Something like that.

Grey Head Boy? Don't be modest. I thought so! Of course I'd left by that time hadn't I?

Haddleton Had you?

Grey Yes. You were Form Captain that year. Come to think of it, you were Form Captain most years! I'll never forget that day you were counting the term's Mission Money. All the form Captains—counting up the silver collection. "For those less fortunate than ourselves" the Head used to say. I thought I could whip a pocketful—all the backs were turned—totting away—one quick grab, that's all I needed to do—then I saw you standing there, watching me—reading my mind. Good old Haddock. Remember what you said?

Haddleton I suppose I said "Don't be so stupid".

Grey Yes. You said "Don't be tempted, Grey. It's not worth it". You saved me. Saved me that time anyway. I remember after that thinking it was always on the cards that you'd be Head Boy or something. I mean you were a bit of a stickler for the rules, weren't you.

Haddleton It's a long time ago. It all seems very trivial now.
Grey Oh I think everything that happened then has some relevance now, don't you?
Haddleton I shouldn't think so.
Grey What about that party you gave—at your house? That wonderful party . . . ?

Haddleton gets up

Haddleton I'm sorry to interrupt this fascinating flow of reminiscence but I must be getting on . . .
Grey Oh. Yes of course. I mustn't keep you. We must have a proper chat sometime. Old Times. Good Luck.
Haddleton Thank you. Good-bye.

Haddleton exits: the Waiter enters

Waiter Mein Herr—your English breakfast—it's ready.
Grey Don't worry Gunter. Better give it to me. I think Herr Haddleton's lost his appetite . . .

Grey smashes the top of his egg with his spoon. The Lights fade to a Black-out. Music

The same evening. The Lights come up on a bedroom in the hotel Haddleton is working at his papers. The telephone buzzes. He picks it up

Haddleton Hello?

As Haddleton answers, a spot comes up on Grey seated at the telephone in the hotel bar

Grey Hello. How was the meeting?
Haddleton Who is this?
Grey I'll give you one guess, Haddock?
Haddleton What do you want?
Grey I just wondered how it was going.
Haddleton How what is going?
Grey Homework, old boy.
Haddleton It's going all right—now if you don't mind . . .

Grey It's a warm evening. Can I tempt you down for a drink?
Haddleton No thanks
Grey All work and no play you know . . .
Haddleton I really don't think so . . .
Grey Can I send you one up?
Haddleton I'm sorry?
Grey A drink. Can I send one up to your room?
Haddleton No, thank you.
Grey What about a beer?
Haddleton Look. Grey. My dear Grey—it's most kind of you,
    but I do not want a drink.
Grey Oh dear. You make me feel guilty.
Haddleton What do you mean?
Grey You sitting up there working your guts out—me sitting
    down here . . . Do you know, I was just laughing to myself
    about that incredible joke . . .
Haddleton What joke?
Grey Don't you remember—at that party of yours. The joke
    with no ending—how you all caught me.
Haddleton Look—for God's sake. Good night.

Haddleton puts down the telephone

The spot goes out on Grey

Jesus. (*He waits a moment, then picks up the telephone again*)
Hello. Hello . . . (*He waits*) Hello. What's the name of that
big hotel—in the centre. By the Town Hall? . . . The Ambassador—yes. Could you get it for me please? . . . Yes—ring
me back will you . . . Thank you. (*He puts the telephone down,
and picks up his papers*) Now . . .

Pause. There is a knock at the door

Yes?

Pause

Who is it?
Grey (*off*) Room Service, sir.
Haddleton Come in.

Grey enters with two steins of beer

Grey Zwi bier, mein herr!
Haddleton What the . . . ? For God's sake—I said I didn't want a drink.
Grey I thought you said you did.
Haddleton I said *no* drink.
Grey My dear fellow. I'm terribly sorry. I thought you said you could do with a drink. I've brought you a beer. I'm terribly sorry, I'll take it downstairs again. (*He starts to go*)
Haddleton No. It's all right. I'll drink it.
Grey No. No. Not if you don't want it—
Haddleton It's all right. I'll drink it.
Grey Well if you're sure.
Haddleton Yes, I'm sure.
Grey That's very decent of you, Haddock. Well cheers, old boy.
Haddleton (*after a moment*) Cheers.

They drink. Pause. Grey moves down towards the audience

Grey You've got a beautiful view from the balcony. I had this room once. Private bath. Balcony. Very nice.
Haddleton Yes.

Haddleton waits for Grey to leave

Grey You know I don't think you should do any more work tonight. You look terrible.
Haddleton Oh. Thanks very much!

Grey indicates a photo-case standing near the bed

Grey Is this your wife?
Haddleton Yes.
Grey Hm. And these are your children?
Haddleton Yes.
Grey On holiday was this?
Haddleton Yes. Last year.
Grey So you're a family man. (*He studies the photos*) Well, well. Amazing. Your wife is very beautiful. Was she a local girl?
Haddleton Yes she was. As a matter of fact I first met Helen in my last year at school, now if you don't mind—
Grey In your last year. That would have been after I—er . . . After my time.

There is a second's pause, then the telephone buzzes. Haddleton answers it

Haddleton Hello?...What? Oh—yes...(*Pause*) Er—no—no —I think there's been some mistake. I'm sorry you've been troubled. Danke. (*He puts down the telephone*)

Grey Wrong room?

Haddleton Wrong room. Well—What do I owe you for the beer?

Grey *Do* you remember that party?

Haddleton Look—I have a lot to do.

Grey No, I must ask you this. Do you remember that party?

Haddleton What party?

Grey Your party. The one you gave. For me.

Haddleton For you? No I certainly don't remember any such party.

Grey Oh but surely. When we were about fifteen. "I'm giving a party," you said. "Like you to come along. My parents will be away. It'll be great fun. Just a few of the mates..."

Haddleton starts pressing his hands together nervously

I thought, how marvellous. The great god has spoken. The Form Captain has smiled upon me. "Just a few of the mates!" But it wasn't quite like that was it? Don't do that. It's all right.

Haddleton I'm not—I'm—I...

Grey What a party. My golly you really set it up well. That absurd drink you produced. Oh, what a brew! "My uncle brought it back from South America," you said. "Oh really," I said, "I think I've had it before. Let me try it..." I tried it. Ugh! Then went out and spewed on the lawn. "I haven't been sick," I said, as I came back in. Snigger snigger from you all. It was concocted by you, of course, out of filth. God, you were brilliant...

Haddleton says nothing

And the Joke. That joke you invented with the punchline that didn't mean anything. All worked out beforehand—You must have spent hours rehearsing. All of you in the know—except for yours truly. You all sat round me. And then you started to tell this so-called funny story. And when you got to the end—

to the meaningless ending—you all fell about, as if it was the funniest, wittiest thing you'd ever heard—and I joined in. Ha. Ha. Ha. Just as you'd hoped. I hadn't a clue what I was laughing at. "At least it's clean," I said, killing myself. "Oh I'm glad *you* think so," you said. A nice touch, that. And you all laughed louder than ever. My own fault though. Too eager to be one of the in-crowd. Without the qualifications. (*Pause*) Do you remember all that?

Haddleton (*moving down to the balcony*) I—I must—must get some air . . .

Grey (*following him*) Haddock—Are you all right? You look a bit sick. Stop doing that.

Haddleton It's the heat. It's very warm.

Grey Yes—in a way that "festive occasion" was the beginning of it all for me. Or the end. It was after that, that I started pinching things from the shops, wasn't it? Remember? Gave me a feeling of superiority I think. Even used to boast about it. Wouldn't learn. Anything to get the attention. Yes, that was the beginning of it. Wouldn't you agree?

Haddleton Yes, O.K. I'm sure this is very interesting, and I'm deeply sorry if you think I should have been nicer to you, but I wonder if you'd give it a rest now. As a matter of fact I'm not feeling too good.

Grey Not too good? Ah! A touch of Foehn perhaps?

Haddleton What?

Grey Foehn. It's a wind. A warm wind from the South. Comes here from the Alps. And it does funny things to you . . . strange things—to Foehn sensitive people—like you. Headaches. Bad temper. Fatigue. Depression.

Haddleton Thank you for your diagnosis. Now perhaps you would be good enough to leave.

Grey You think I'm joking? Its effect can be pretty widespread. Look down there. A court of law here will even consider Foehn in mitigation when it's passing sentence. It's a fact, Haddock. For instance if you were to push me over this balcony now, you could plead Foehn in mitigation. No really. And so could I—if I were to push you. I'd only have to stretch out my hand. (*He is only a yard away from Haddleton. He slowly reaches out and places his hand against the side of Haddleton's shoulder*) Yes. It's a funny thing. (*Pause. He* *moves away*) Well I think you should get to bed. Another big day tomorrow haven't you? Don't worry about the drink. It's my treat. I'll go out this way. Along the balcony—it runs right round. We'll er—continue another time, eh? Good night.

Grey goes

Haddleton picks up the telephone

Haddleton Hello. Hello. (*He taps the rest*) Hello . . . Sorry. Get me the Ambassador Hotel again please . . . Yes, I'll hold on . . . Thank you. (*Pause*) Come on. Come on. (*He waits*) Oh good evening. Have you by any chance a room with a private bath? Oh—as soon as possible please. Tomorrow. And for the rest of the week. (*Pause*) Nothing? Nothing at all? Oh yes. I see. The festival. I just wondered. Right. Thank you. (*He puts down the telephone*) **Bugger!**

The Lights fade to a Black-out. Music

The following afternoon. The Lights come up on the bar. Grey is sitting at it. Dietl enters

Grey Hello, Herr Dietl. Looking for Roger?
Dietl No I've just left him. He is in his room. He is not well.
Grey Really? I'm sorry to hear that. Too much schnapps at lunch?
Dietl No, no. We were showing him round one of our factories and he fainted—collapsed. Just the heat, I think. The noise of the machines.
Grey Dear, dear. A bit unfortunate—eh? At such a time. It's all fairly crucial isn't it?
Dietl Unfortunate? Yes—maybe . . .
Grey Well—I'll be seeing you.
Dietl Oh, Mister Grey—moment please. Forgive me—I wonder . . . (*He pauses*) No, it's nothing.
Grey I'll look in on Roger later. See how he is . . .
Dietl No. Don't do that, Mister Grey. He'll be O.K.
Grey It's no trouble old boy. He's an old friend.
Dietl Yes. But there's no need. Let him alone. Please. Good evening, Mister Grey.

Dietl goes

The Lights fade to a Black-out

*The Lights come up on the bedroom. Haddleton is seated there.
Grey knocks and enters*

Grey Hallo, Haddock.
Haddleton What do you want?
Grey I've just heard the bad news. I gather you had a bit of a
   turn.
Haddleton I'm perfectly all right.
Grey Are you? Can you subtract seven from a hundred?
Haddleton Don't be absurd.
Grey Start at a hundred and go back to one, taking off seven
   each time. Go on. See if you can do it. That'll tell you how
   you are.
Haddleton For god's sake.
Grey All right, forget it. At any rate, I think you should take it
   easy. Difficult of course at a time like this. Anything I can do?
Haddleton You can get out.
Grey My dear fellow. I should get some shut-eye if I were you.
   I'll look in again later.
Haddleton No thank you.
Grey Well sleep tight. (*He turns to go*)
Haddleton Grey . . .
Grey Yes, Haddock?

Pause

Haddleton Don't call me that.
Grey Oh, sorry.
Haddleton We were never friends at school. I don't see any point
   in pretending we were.
Grey Oh I was a great fan of yours. You know that.
Haddleton It was a very long time ago.
Grey I haven't forgotten. I don't forget that easily, Haddock.
   Sorry—Roger. (*He picks up the photo case*) Your wife really is
   extraordinarily pretty. Where did you say this was taken?

Silence

Haddleton Look . . .
Grey Where?
Haddleton Tunisia. Last year.
Grey Did you take it?
Haddleton Yes. I managed to join them for the last ten days.
Grey Nice for Helen. Well, I'll leave you to your shut-eye. (*He starts to go*)
Haddleton How do you know my wife's name?
Grey (*stopping*) You told me. Last night. You really do have a shocking memory.
Haddleton I told you?
Grey Yes. When you said she was a local girl. (*He picks up the photos again*) Although I do remember her, as a matter of fact. She always had those eyes. The kind of eyes men dream about. She was at the High School, wasn't she. I remember those terrible dances, when we all had to be introduced to the Head mistress. Or did you never go? I suppose you'd have been too busy with your rugger practice anyway. Scrumming down and getting it out! Yes I remember Helen. She was always very nice to me. Of course I never really had a chance, with all you rugby chaps.
Haddleton Look—what are you trying to do?
Grey Can you take seven from a hundred?
Haddleton Oh please . . . Get out. Get out.
Grey All right, all right. I'll see you. There's still a lot to say. 'Bye now.

Grey goes

Haddleton Bastard. Bloody bastard. (*He goes to the telephone*) Hello. Hello . . . Oh—please, would you get me a number in England. It's a London number. You can dial it direct. It's o-one, one-two-two, o-seven-six-nine . . . Yes . . . No. I'll hold on. Get it for me quickly please. (*Pause*) Thank you. Bastard. Hundred minus seven—ninety-three—minus seven is —eighty—eighty—six? Yes, eighty-six. . . . (*He listens, then hears the ringing tone begin*) Ah. (*He waits*) Come on—come on—minus seven—is seventy—seventy—what is it? Seventy . . . ? Come on, Helen . . . (*There is no reply*) Seventy what . . . ?

The Lights fade to a Black-out. Music

The Lights come up on the bedroom. Haddleton is on the bed, asleep. Grey enters from the balcony. He waits, perhaps sits, and watches Haddleton. Eventually Haddleton opens his eyes and sees Grey

Grey (*quietly*) Hello, Haddock.

Pause

Haddleton What do you want?
Grey Hello, Haddock. Did I make you jump?
Haddleton How long have you been here?
Grey A long time. I've been watching you.
Haddleton I locked the door . . .
Grey I came along the balcony. It's a beautiful night. I've brought you some Schnapps.
Haddleton (*rising*) I don't want any. Get out.
Grey Come on. 'My uncle brought it back from South America' —eh? Joke, Haddock (*He pours out the Schnapps*)
Haddleton For God's sake—do I have to get them to throw you out.
Grey You won't, you know. Go on. It's only Schnapps. You may need it.
Haddleton All right. What do you want? (*He takes the glass*)
Grey Drink with me and I'll tell you. (*He raises his own glass*) Prosit! (*He drinks*)

Haddleton mutters "Prosit", and drinks

Do you remember the wonderful affair of the Moving Desks? When *you* broke the rules. It was your scheme. All those in Five-A breaking into the school after dark and shifting the masters' desks around. Old Rags' desk up to Ding Dong's room. Treacle-pants' desk down to the Art room. Room one's desk to room sixteen, at the other side of the Quad. Marvellous. I'll never forget that first lesson next morning. Slow dawning of chaos as master after master discovered he was sitting behind another master's desk. Took them days to get it sorted out. And nobody had the remotest idea who'd done it. You do remember.

Haddleton Yes. I remember. It was extremely well planned and carried out.

Grey Of course.

Haddleton I'd forgotten you were involved in that.

Grey I wasn't.

Haddleton You weren't?

Grey I wasn't asked. Everybody in Five-A except me.

Haddleton Then—how did you—?

Grey How did I know? When nobody was supposed to know. Oh, I knew.

Haddleton I can't really remember now . . .

Grey No, you didn't ask me. Only those who could be relied upon to pull their weight. Still it was a wonderful scheme. Went down in the history of the school. Not perhaps quite the sort of thing expected of a Five Percenter, trespassing—although I don't know—leaders of men and all that. A great triumph anyway. Even if it was against the rules.

Haddleton Why are you telling me all this? It's another world. It's over—gone.

Grey Not for me. Or you, *now*.

Pause

Haddleton You've obviously been harbouring all this for years. What now? So what?

Grey You know, you really mustn't be so vulnerable. Stop doing that with your hands—you'll break your glass.

Haddleton You've—you've said nothing about . . .

Grey Yes? Go on. About what?

Haddleton I know what this is all about.

Grey You do?

Haddleton Yes. But everything you did was your own fault. You said that yourself. It wasn't my fault. It's yours. Bloody yours. You had nobody to blame but yourself for what happened. O.K. maybe we were bastards to you. Maybe I did go a bit far at that party, but Christ you bloody deserved it. Slimy little sod—always trying to muscle in, get in on our act. O.K. So you started pinching things to get the attention. Poor little boy. Poor little non-games playing weed.

Grey Have some more Schnapps!

Haddleton (*knocking the bottle aside and continuing*) But nobody was bloody interested in you. I tried to help you . . .
Grey Yes, you did. Over the Mission Money. You saved me over that. No you were a great figure at school. An inspiration to others. That's the phrase isn't it? "He exerted a very real influence in the form". I bet your reports used to say that. "Moral Tone: High". Go on, drink up. It was kindness you did. On that occasion. Pity I didn't learn from it. Wasn't it.
Haddleton What do you mean?
Grey The match against The County Club and Ground . . . Funny how we pin down our memories. Yes, that was the day— I let you down. Wasn't it? In the end? Haddock?
Haddleton Please go. Go away . . .
Grey I let you down. Isn't that how you see it? "Lack of moral fibre". Ever since the Headmaster had made that announcement in Prayers: "A number of boys have had money taken from the changing rooms. All team changing rooms are out of bounds, except to members of Teams. You are all of you on your honour to report anybody breaking this rule—And if anybody knows who the culprit is . . ." etcetera etcetera. On your honour . . . Mind you—you'd got me marked down I'm sure—I mean with my record, who could blame you. And then the afternoon of the match: hundred before lunch—my god we were proud of you that day. You went into your changing room —the First Eleven Changing room—whiter than white in your flannels—and there I was. Haddock, I'll never forget your face when you saw me. Noble outrage. Trespassers will be . . . You see I thought you were all at tea—in the pavilion . . .
Haddleton I came back to fetch my blazer . . .
Grey Which I was wearing. Oh my God—caught in the act. Wearing your blazer—in all its bright gold trimmed glory. First Eleven Blazer. Just to see what it felt like—and you said. . . .
Haddleton (*slowly*) "What the bloody hell do you think you're doing?"
Grey Please don't tell. Oh please, Haddleton. Please let me off— I wasn't doing any harm. Just came to see what it was like. I wasn't going to take anything. I haven't taken any money. It wasn't me. Oh please Haddleton. Please give me a chance. They'll chuck me out. Please don't go to the Head. Please . . .

Haddleton (*quietly*) Please—don't . . .

Grey But you had to. Didn't you?

Haddleton It was my duty.

Grey Nelson House—England expects . . . Your duty—as a good Form Captain.

Haddleton Goddamit, you were breaking the rules! You shouldn't have been in the room anyway. Our room. First Eleven Changing room. I don't care whether you were the thief or not—you were bloody capable of it—and I bet you did take it—wearing my blazer. First Eleven blazer, other people's property, trespassing. You shouldn't have been in there—You'd no right to be in there. Our changing room. First Eleven Changing room. You were breaking the rules.

Silence

Grey Of course I was. (*He refills Haddleton's glass*) To be expelled is a terrible thing you know Haddock. Expulsion. Rejected by the community—even when you've never really felt a part of it. You never quite recover. Never quite catch up again. No "O" levels, no top five-per-cent jobs. And of course the guilt. They make you feel guilty, so you are. And of course I'd been guilty all those other times—in Woolworth's—and I once did a bit of scrumping in the Art room—pinched a pile of rotten fruit . . . Oh, yes it was fair to tell the Head about all those other times. You were fair. Very fair. (*He drinks some Schnapps*) Everything else drains away. Except the guilt. That's always there somewhere. (*He moves a pace towards Haddleton*)

Pause

Haddleton Yes. I know. (*Moving away on to the balcony*) All my life, since that time, I've dreaded seeing you again. Dreaded it. I mean—I'm a different person now—and yet it was still me, the same me, who—who took you to the Head. Because of me . . . they chucked you out.

Grey follows Haddleton on to the balcony

    I once saw you in the distance on Charing Cross Station, years ago—soon after I'd left. And I knew then that I could never—never speak to you . . . it would never be all right . . . that in this respect at least, I was still a boy, not a man. (*He drinks some more Schnapps*) And the other evening in the bar. I knew it was you the second I saw you. (*Pause*) Well, there you are. I've said it—it's over. You've had your revenge, is that it? Thrown me completely. I've messed up this deal—I shall lose that contract tomorrow, and probably my job. Ten out of ten. So what else. What now. What more do you want?

Grey says nothing. He moves nearer to Haddleton, who remains still, pressing his glass between his palms

Grey (*quietly*) It's a beautiful view from up here. I only have to stretch out my hand . . .

As Grey's hand touches Haddleton's shoulder there is a crack as Haddleton's glass smashes between his hands and falls to the floor. Grey breaks the silence

My dear fellow, you've got blood on your fingers. I told you that would happen. You really must stop doing that with your hands.

Haddleton remains motionless

Grey I think you'd better come inside. Come on. Come in.

They go in

Now let's have a look. Mm, it's not much. You'd better take this—(*he gives Haddleton his handkerchief*)—wrap it round . . . All right? Well, back to bed for you I think. Come on. Beddy-bumps, old boy.

Haddleton sits on the bed

Jolly good. Now you get some rest. You hear me? You've been overdoing it a bit. Still, you'll probably feel a lot better to-morrow. All things considered.

Haddleton (*after a moment*) Grey . . .

Grey Yes?

Haddleton You know, I really thought—I thought you'd got it in for me . . .

Grey Did you old boy? Whatever gave you that idea? Lights out, eh? (*He turns out the light and stands for a moment by the bed and sings gently*)

When across the world are scattered,
As old boys we'll raise the cry . . .

Well, sleep tight. (*He starts to go—then pauses*) Thought I had
it in for you eh? That would hardly be fair—hardly cricket . . .
And anyway—it's against the rules . . . (*He sings*)
   Honour, honour, truth and honour,
   Truth and honour till we die.
Bye—Haddock.

Grey goes

The Lights fade to a Black-out and the music swells.

FURNITURE AND PROPERTY LIST

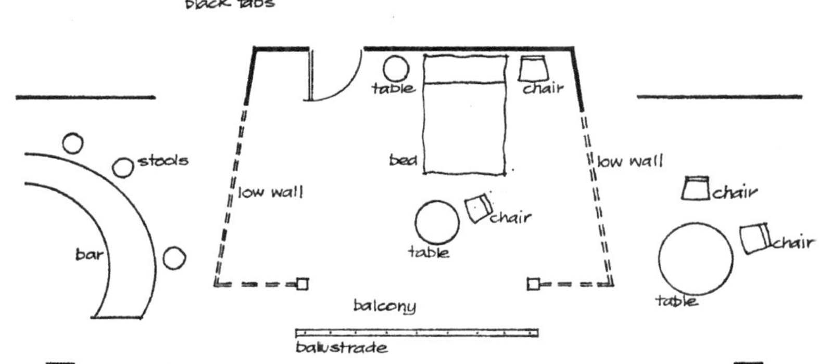

On stage: **BAR:**
Curved bar. *On it:* 3 steins of beer, telephone, ashtrays, beer
mats and general dressing
3 bar stools

BEDROOM:
Bed and bedding
Bed table. *On it:* family photos in case
2 small chairs
Circular table. *On it:* papers, pens, telephone, briefcase

DINING-ROOM:
Circular table. *On it:* cloth. 2 cups, 2 saucers, 2 spoons,
sugarbowl, basket of rolls, butter, butter knife, preserve,
cruet
2 small chairs

Off stage: Tray with coffee jug and cream **(Waiter)**
Tray with egg, egg spoon, toast in rack **(Waiter)**
2 steins of beer **(Grey)**
Bottle of Schnapps and 2 steins **(Grey)**

Personal: **Grey:** handkerchief

Black-out changes:

Haddleton: "I don't remember him, you know."   (Page 6)
Strike dirty steins from bar

Haddleton: "Bugger."   (Page 14)
*Set stein of beer on bar. Strike steins from
bedroom*

Dietl exits   (Page 15)
Strike stein from bar

LIGHTING PLOT

Property fittings required: 1 bedroom wall light
Interiors. A composite set

To open:	Black-out	
Cue 1	As action starts *Bring up bar lighting*	(Page 1)
Cue 2	**Haddleton:** "I don't remember him, you know." *Fade to Black-out. Bring up dining-room lighting*	(Page 6)
Cue 3	**Grey** smashes egg top *Fade to Black-out. Bring up bedroom lighting,* *including bed light*	(Page 9)
Cue 4	Telephone buzzes *Bring up spot on* **Grey** *at bar*	(Page 9)
Cue 5	**Haddleton** puts down phone *Spot off*	(Page 10)
Cue 6	**Haddleton:** "Bugger." *Fade to Black-out. Bring up bar lighting*	(Page 14)
Cue 7	**Dietl** exits *Fade to Black-out. Bring up bedroom lighting*	(Page 15)
Cue 8	**Haddleton:** "Seventy what . . .?" *Fade to Black-out, then return to previous lighting* *when* **Haddleton** *on bed*	(Page 16)
Cue 9	**Grey** turns out light *Snap off bed light and covering spots*	(Page 21)
Cue 10	**Grey** exits *Fade to Black-out*	(Page 22)

EFFECTS PLOT

www.ingramcontent.com/pod-product-compliance
Ingram Content Group UK Ltd.
Pitfield, Milton Keynes, MK11 3LW, UK
UKHW021820150726
7214IPUK00017B/232